A First Book of
CLASSICAL MUSIC

FOR THE BEGINNING PIANIST with DOWNLOADABLE MP3s

Bergerac

DOVER PUBLICATIONS, INC.
Mineola, New York

All songs available as downloadable MP3s!

Go to: http://www.doverpublications.com/0486780090
to access these files.

Bibliographical Note

A First Book of Classical Music for the Beginning Pianist with Downloadable MP3s,
first published by Dover Publications, Inc., in 2013, is a revised edition of *A First
Book of Classical Music: 29 Themes by Beethoven, Mozart, Chopin and Other Great
Composers in Easy Piano Arrangements,* originally published by Dover in 2000.

International Standard Book Number

ISBN-13: 978-0-486-78009-2
ISBN-10: 0-486-78009-0

Manufactured in the United States by LSC Communications
78009005   2019
www.doverpublications.com

CONTENTS

ITALIAN WORDS IN THE MUSIC

adagio cantabile, very slow and songful

allegretto, moving along, but not too fast

allegro passionato, fast and impassioned

andante, walking tempo

andante grazioso, walking tempo
    in a graceful manner

andantino, a bit faster than a walking tempo

a tempo, return to the original speed

coda, "tail piece," a concluding section

cresc(endo), getting louder

dim. e rit. (diminuendo e ritardando) poco a poco,
    gradually quieter and slower

D. C. al Fine (da capo al fine), return to the
    beginning, then go to the sign "Fine" (end)

dolce, gently, sweetly

espressivo, espr., expressive

fine, end

f *(forte)*, loud

ff *(fortissimo)*, very loud

fz *(forzando)*, strongly accented

ffz *(molto forzando)*, very strongly accented

largo, very slow, solemn

legato, smooth, connected

leggiero, lightly

lento, very slow (a bit faster than *largo*)

lento espressivo, slow and expressive

L.H., left hand

marc(ato), marked, accented

mf *(mezzo-forte)*, medium loud

moderato, at a moderate speed

molto marcato, very accented

molto rit(ardando), slow down a great deal

molto staccato, very short and detached

mp *(mezzo-piano)*, medium soft

p *(piano)*, soft

pp *(pianissimo)*, very soft

poco a poco, little by little

poco rall(entando), slightly held back

poco rit(ardando), slowing down a little

rall(entando), held back

rall. poco a poco, held back little by little

R.H., right hand

sfz *(sforzando)*, strongly accented

sostenuto, sost., sustained

Johann Sebastian Bach
(Germany, 1685–1750)
MINUET

Bach's young wife, Anna Magdalena, brought great happiness to his household. Together
they kept little notebooks that were full of the most miscellaneous matters, including the
manuscript of this graceful minuet that he composed for her in 1722, when he was 37
years old. Such court dances were extremely popular among the nobility of Europe.

Pay attention to the hand position shifts

RH only to start 11/7/21

Johann Sebastian Bach
SHEEP MAY SAFELY GRAZE

Five years before his marriage to Anna, Bach wrote special music for the birthday of Duke Christian, celebrated in the form of a great hunting festival. The singers played roles from ancient mythology, including Pales (pronounced *Pah-less*) the goddess of flocks and herds. This is her lovely, serene aria, singing about the free, open-air life of shepherds and their flocks.

Gently flowing

Ludwig van Beethoven

(Germany, 1770–1827)

ODE TO JOY

In the year 1822—exactly 100 years after Bach composed his gentle minuet for Anna (see p. 5)—Beethoven solved the troublesome problem of how to end his colossal Symphony No. 9. It would be a musical setting for full chorus of "Ode to Joy," a poem by Friedrich Schiller: *"Joy, we are under your divine spell. All men become brothers wherever joy is found . . ."*

In a steady march-like rhythm

Ludwig van Beethoven
MINUET IN G

This charming court dance is one of Beethoven's most famous pieces. Despite his reputation for lengthy, dramatic compositions, the composer was also fond of writing such short dance music as *éccossaises* (in Scottish style), *allemandes* (in German style), and country dances called *Ländler* and *contredanses*. He composed the Minuet in G about 1795, when he was 25 years old.

Andantino

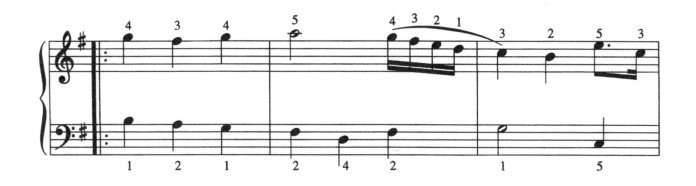

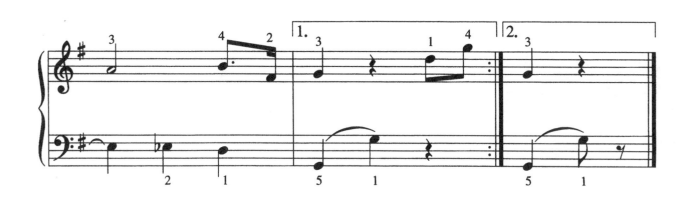

9

Johannes Brahms

(Germany, 1833–1897)

HUNGARIAN DANCE NO. 5

In 1848, when he was 15, a stream of Hungarian rebels passed through Brahms's hometown of Hamburg on their way to America. Some stayed on, bringing their music with them, starting a national craze for the wild, passionate music of the Hungarian Gypsies. Four years later, Brahms began to compose 21 Hungarian Dances, recalling those wonderful tunes and rhythms.

A little slower and lyrical

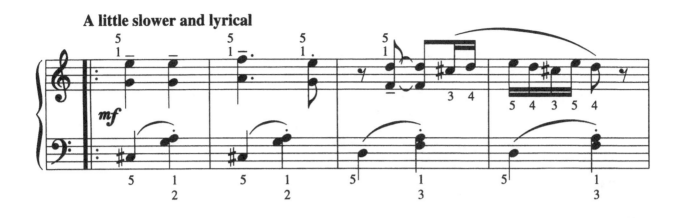

gradually slower _ _ _ _ _ _ _ _ _ _ _ _

held back, lingering and sentimental _ _ _ _ _ _ _ _ _ _ _   *a tempo*

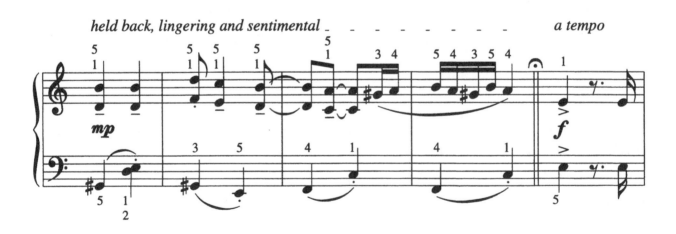

D.C. al Fine

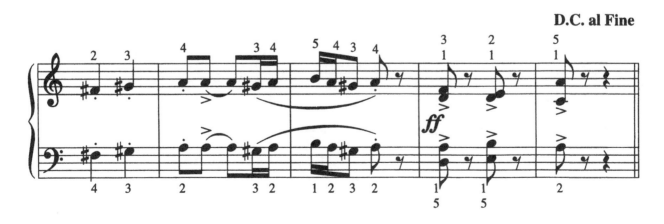

Frédéric Chopin

(Poland and France, 1810–1849)

NOCTURNE

Piano composers in the 19th century were fond of giving fanciful, often meaningless, names to their pieces—such as "rhapsody," "impromptu," "album leaf," "intermezzo," "fantasy" and so on. Chopin liked the French word "nocturne" (night piece) for 21 piano pieces composed in a dreamy mood. This one (Opus 9, No. 2) is his most famous nocturne, full of beautiful melody.

Andante

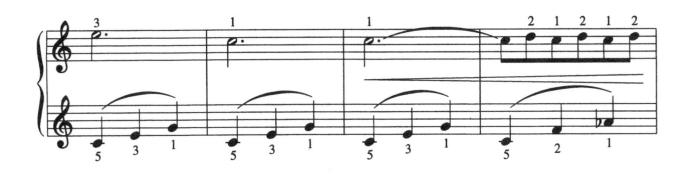

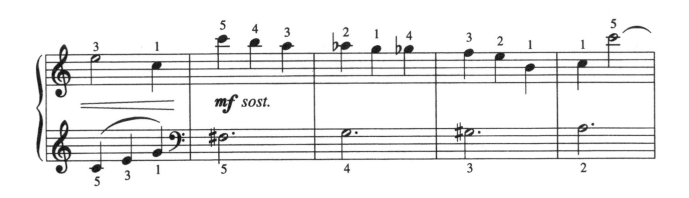

gradually dying away till the end

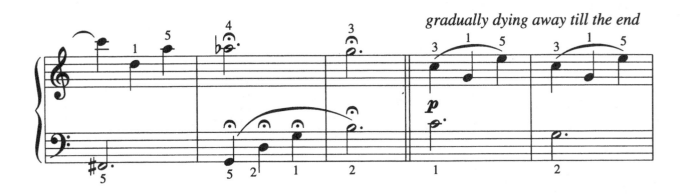

Muzio Clementi

(Italy, 1752–1832)

RONDO IN C

(From Sonata in C, Op. 36, No. 1)

It's hard to imagine Clementi's sensational career: keyboard virtuoso, teacher, conductor, composer, publisher (he had a contract with Beethoven), and piano manufacturer trading as Clementi & Company, London. Travelling all over Europe and Russia, he even performed in a piano contest before European royalty. (His opponent, believe it or not, was *Mozart* himself.)

Lightly

Antonín Dvořák

(Czechoslovakia, 1841–1904)

FROM THE NEW WORLD

(Slow theme from the second movement of Symphony No. 9, Op. 95)

Dvořák was 51 when he was invited to America as director of a New York music conservatory. He arrived with his family for a three-year stay, spending their summers in a Czech community in Iowa. There, in 1893, he completed his Symphony "From the New World." The song "Goin' Home," with words by William Arms Fisher (1922), was based on Dvořák's original slow theme for the second movement. It was not a Negro spiritual, as some people believed.

Stephen C. Foster

(United States, 1826–1864)

BEAUTIFUL DREAMER

(His 'last song ever written' / 1864)

In a life cut tragically short (he died in poverty at age 38), Stephen Collins Foster wrote about 200 songs. Many are so well-known, and have been around for such a long time, that we think of them as genuine folk songs. His famous "My Old Kentucky Home" became the offical state song of Kentucky, and his beloved "Old Folks at Home" was chosen as Florida's state song.

A slow serenade

Edvard Grieg

(Norway, 1843–1907)

MORNING MOOD

Grieg loved his native Norway, pouring the sounds and feelings of its folk songs and dances into his music. At the age of 31, Grieg was invited by the famous Norwegian playwright Henrik Ibsen to write "incidental" music to accompany his play *Peer Gynt.* "Morning Mood," "Anitra's Dance" and "In the Hall of the Mountain King" are three world-famous selections from that fine music.

George Frideric Handel

(Germany & England, 1685–1759)

SARABANDE

Did you know that Johann Sebastian Bach, Domenico Scarlatti and Handel were all born in the same year (1685)? All three were not only great composers, but phenomenal keyboard virtuosos as well. They wrote and performed some of the greatest, most popular harpsichord music ever composed. This stately court dance is from Handel's Suite in D minor for harpsichord, published in 1720.

Joseph Haydn

(Austria, 1732–1809)

SONATA IN C

(First movement of Sonata No. 35 / 1780)

History says that young Haydn was a lively boy who loved practical jokes. As a young man, however, he had a hard time supporting himself, teaching a bit, performing a lot, and composing continually to make a living. Today, he is honored as "father" of the classical sonata and the symphony (he wrote 104 of them) . . . and his list of works fills over 40 pages of the music encyclopedia!

Lively, with good spirit

19

Joseph Haydn
"SURPRISE" SYMPHONY

The popular story goes that Haydn wanted "to wake up the ladies" by shocking his audience with an unexpected drum stroke played *forte*. This "surprise" occurs in the otherwise peaceful slow movement of his Symphony No. 94. This tuneful work is one of the composer's so-called "London" symphonies—twelve works written for concerts he gave in London, from 1791 to 1795.

Edward MacDowell
(United States, 1860–1908)

TO A WILD ROSE

The American Edward MacDowell was a lot like the Norwegian Edvard Grieg. They lived at the same time, they were both fine pianists, and both were at their best writing miniature pieces about nature and homeland. MacDowell's gentle "To a Wild Rose," composed in 1896, is from his *Woodland Sketches*. Three other popular suites are called *Fireside Tales, New England Idylls*, and *Sea Pieces*.

Franz Liszt

(Hungary & Germany, 1811–1886)

HUNGARIAN RHAPSODY NO. 2

Liszt was the great superstar of the 19th century. Considered by some to be the best pianist who ever lived, he was honored by kings and adored by the public who flocked to his sold-out concerts throughout Europe and Russia. They especially loved to hear Liszt play his own pieces based on the sad tunes and wild dances of the gypsy bands that traveled throughout his native Hungary.

Very lively and dynamic

gradually pulling back, bigger and broader

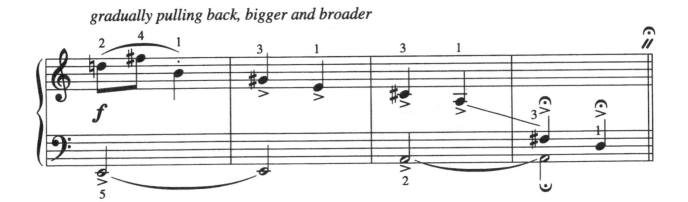

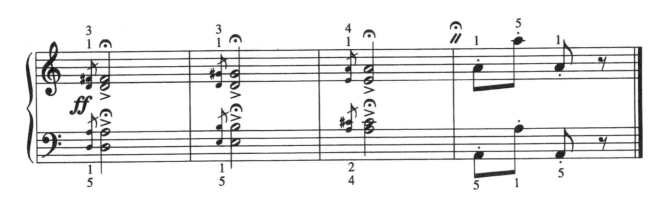

Wolfgang Amadeus Mozart

(Austria, 1756–1791)

PAPAGENO'S SONG

You may think opera is stuffy—but then you haven't heard Mozart's fairy-tale "singing play" called *The Magic Flute*! It has a prince, a girl he has to rescue, a wizard, a magic flute, and a comical bird-catcher called Papageno. "Yes, I am the birdcatcher," he sings, "always cheerful, well-known every-where! If only I could catch a sweet young girl so that she'd be all mine! I'd feed her on sugar!"

Bright and bouncy

(The right hand tells its own story)

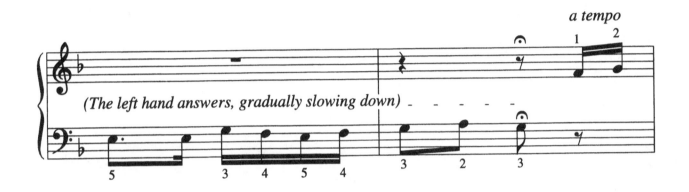

a tempo

(The left hand answers, gradually slowing down)

(a light-hearted duet)

25

Wolfgang Amadeus Mozart
ROMANZE

"Romanze" is the German spelling of *romance*—in music, the name for a gentle and lyrical piece that is very melodious, with a tender character. This *Romanze* is the slow movement of Mozart's popular Piano Concerto No. 20. Did you know that this great composer (who lived over 200 years ago) was also a wonderful pianist? He first performed in public at the age of 5—and could even play blindfolded!

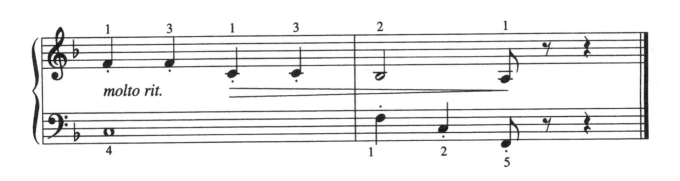

Ignacy Jan Paderewski

(Poland, 1860–1941)

MINUET IN OLDEN STYLE

Can you imagine a superstar music celebrity becoming *head* of the country? Strange as it seems, that's what happened to pianist-composer Ignacy Paderewski at the age of 59. Using his worldwide reputation as a great performer, he raised money for Polish victims of World War I and for Polish liberation. In 1919, he became Poland's Prime Minister and helped sign the Treaty of Versailles that ended the war. Paderewski played this extremely popular, very charming Minuet all over the world.

Jean-Philippe Rameau

(France, 1683–1764)

TAMBOURIN

Rameau was composing in France when America was still a group of colonies governed by the King of England. Although he wrote 33 little operas and ballets, and many miniatures for harpsichord (the "grandfather" of the modern piano), he was proudest of his many books on music theory. The *tambourin* of this lively piece was a long, narrow drum from southern France, near Spain. It is *not* a tambourine!

Serge Rachmaninoff

(Russia & United States, 1873–1943)

PRELUDE

Some call this mighty Prelude by the name "The Bells of Moscow." Those powerful left-hand tones—long and accented—do suggest the tolling of large church bells. But notice that the right-hand "echos" are always subdued and plaintive, like a quiet afterthought. Although Rachmaninoff wrote 24 Preludes, this is the one his worldwide audiences demanded at every piano recital he played. This popular composer-pianist lived till the age of 70, but wrote this piece when he was only 20 years old.

Lento

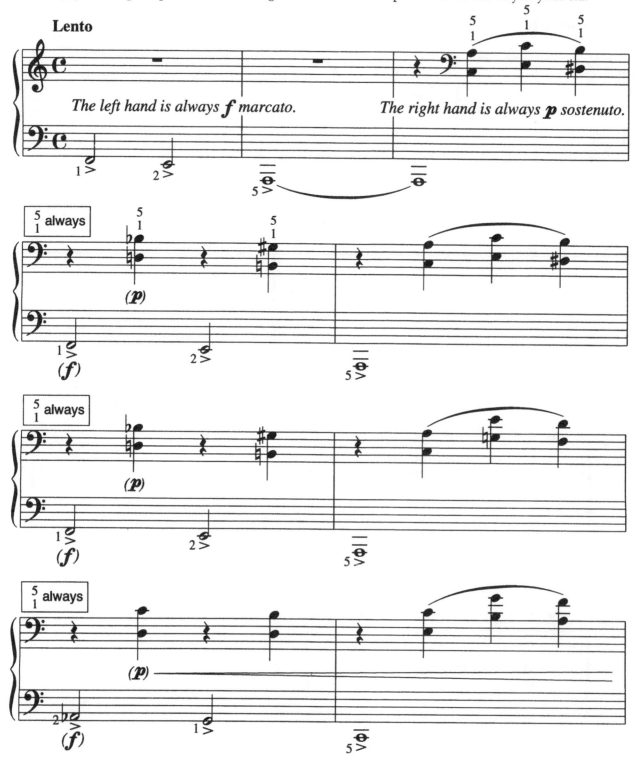

31

Anton Rubinstein
(Russia, 1829–1894)

MELODY IN F

Some say that Rubinstein looked like a lion, but played like an angel. He lived at the same time as the great Franz Liszt, and was considered *almost* as great a pianist as that Hungarian virtuoso. Although Rubinstein composed many piano pieces and five mighty piano concertos, he is remembered almost exclusively for this simple *Melody in F*. Some know the tune as the song "Welcome, Sweet Springtime."

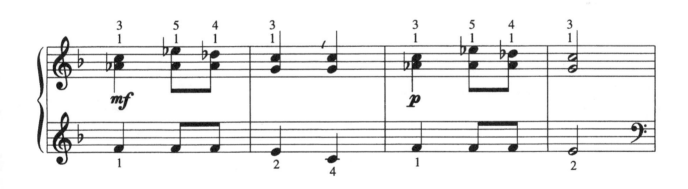

D.C. al Fine

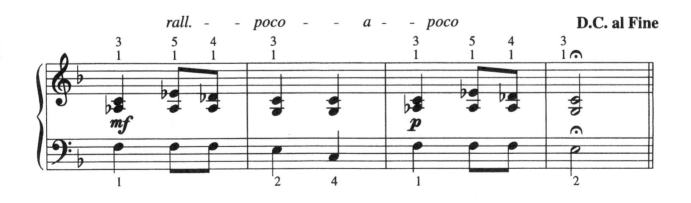

Camille Saint-Saëns
(France, 1835–1921)

THE SWAN

Intended as a musical joke, Saint-Saëns' *The Carnival of the Animals* was dashed off in a few days while the composer was on vacation in February 1886. "The Swan" was always a highlight of the 14 pieces he called his "grand zoological fantasy." Notice how it perfectly captures the feeling of an elegant swan floating on a still lake. (Pronounce this French composer's name *ka-mee san–sawn*.)

Adagio cantabile

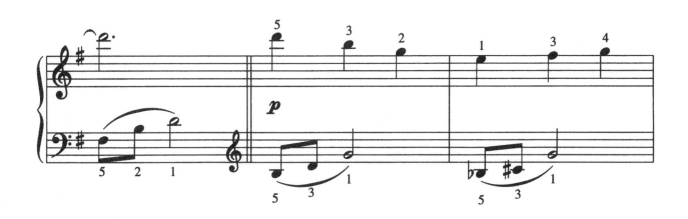

(turn) →

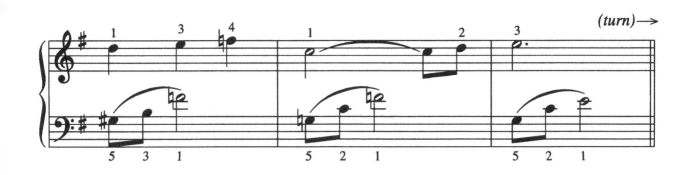

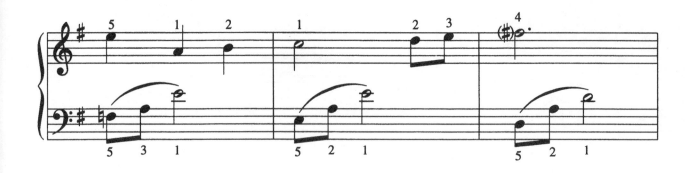

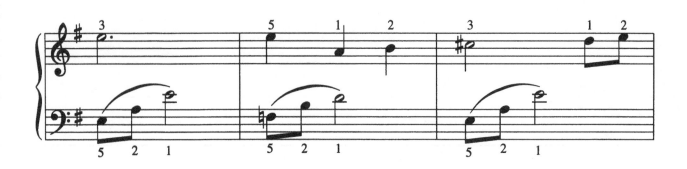

poco rit. - - - - - - - - - - - - - *a tempo*

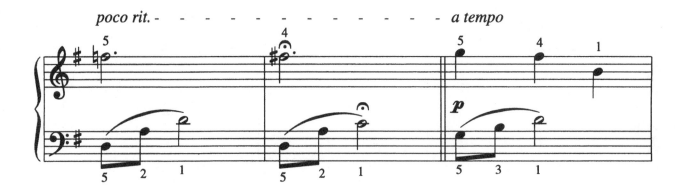

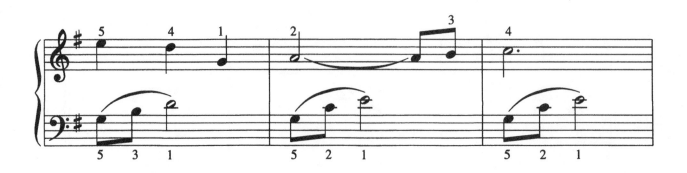

gradually relaxing until the quiet end

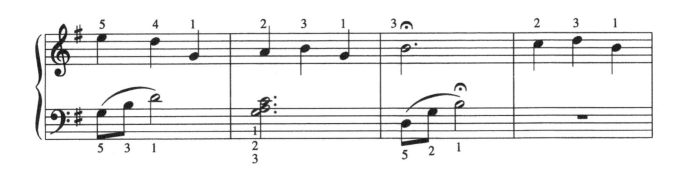

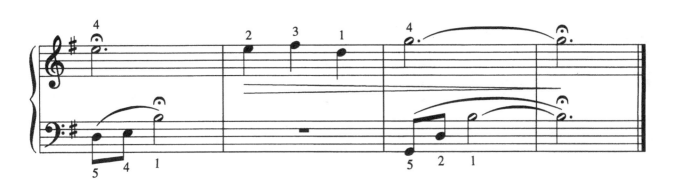

Franz Schubert

(Austria, 1797–1828)

THE TROUT

"The Trout" was originally a short poem about a hasty fish about to be hooked by a patient fisherman. Schubert loved this verse so much that he first set it to music as a song for voice and piano. Two years later, at age 22, he borrowed his own melody for a "theme-and-variations" movement composed for piano, violin, viola, cello and string bass. Naturally, this famous piece is called the "Trout" Quintet.

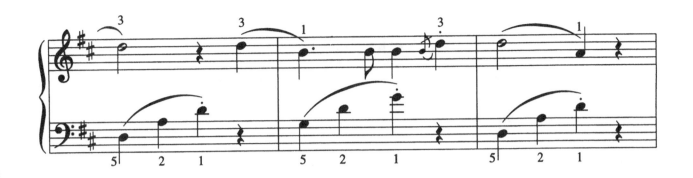

Coda: *slightly slower*

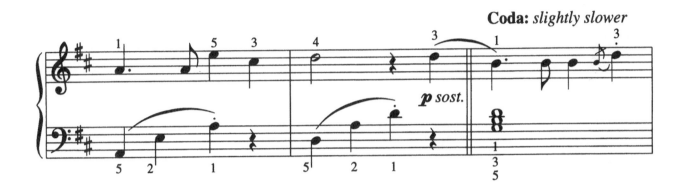

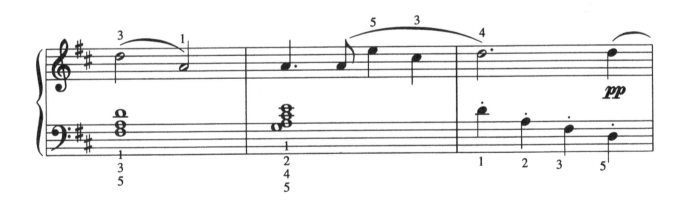

Robert Schumann

(Germany, 1810–1856)

TRÄUMEREI

(From *Scenes from Childhood*, Op. 15 / 1838)

The fact that Clara and Robert Schumann had *eight* children may have something to do with Robert's devotion to children's music—a rarity among 19th-century composers. He composed his *Album for the Young* for beginning players, and *Scenes from Childhood* for *all* pianists. "Träumerei" means "revery," describing a dreamy moment in a child's life. Play it gently (*dolce*), but without dragging the tempo.

Robert Schumann
THE HAPPY FARMER
(From *Album for the Young*, Op. 68 / 1848)

Here's a delightful piece from the suite that Schumann composed for beginning pianists. He finished all 43 miniatures in only two weeks, and gave the first seven pieces to his daughter Marie as a gift for her seventh birthday. The full title of this piece is "The Happy Farmer Returning from Work"—a good clue for playing it. Like the farmer coming home again, it should be full of joy.

Johann Strauss, Jr.

(Austria, 1825–1899)

PIZZICATO POLKA

(Written with his brother Josef / 1870)

You cannot imagine how popular Johann and his dance orchestra was! His adoring public filled every ballroom he played in, sought tickets to every sold-out concert he gave throughout Europe and Russia, and bought copies of every dance piece he composed. No wonder he was called "King of the Waltz"! "Pizzicato" means "plucked string"—a good guide for playing all those short, light *staccato* notes.

Introduction: *Hesitant and playful*

Playful and light

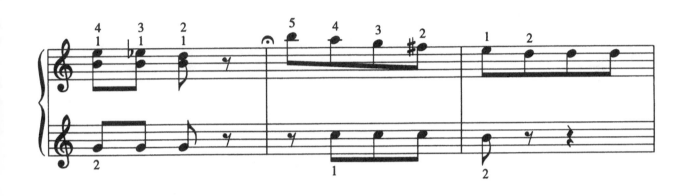

slightly held back till repeat

Peter Ilyitch Tchaikovsky

(Russia, 1840–1893)

MARCHE SLAVE

Tchaikovsky loved the music of the many peoples that lived in and near the vast boundaries of his native Russia. The Slavs were the most numerous of these groups, coming from Russia, Poland, Czechoslovakia, Serbia and other neighboring countries. This *Marche Slave* ('slave' is pronounced *slahv*) means "Slavonic March" and is based on a Serbian folksong.

Slow march

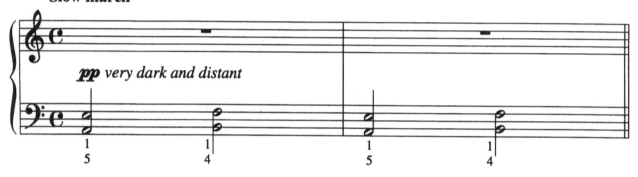

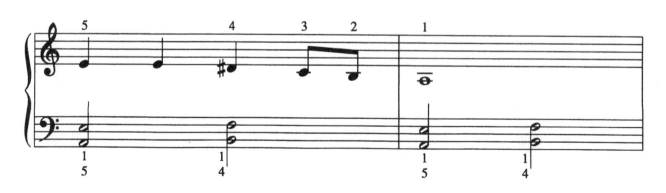

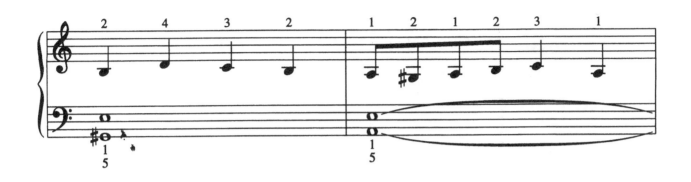

gradually slower till the end, dying away

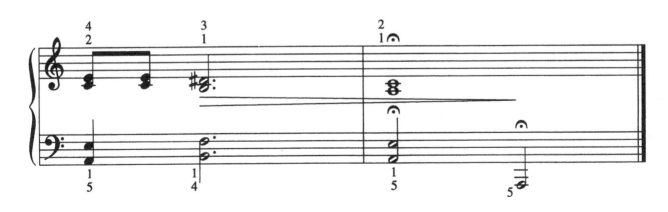

Richard Wagner

(Germany, 1813–1883)

SONG TO THE EVENING STAR

Tannhäuser is a medieval knight whose feelings are torn between pleasure and prayer, not knowing which way to turn. Wagner composed an opera named after him (pronounced *tahn-hoy-zer*) which is still performed throughout the world. This lovely song to the evening star is sung by Tannhäuser's friend as he waits patiently for the lost, confused knight.

Lento espressivo

cresc. poco a poco - - - - - - - - - - - - -

mf *dim. e rit. poco* - - - -

a - - - *poco* - - - - - - - - - - - *pp*

Antonio Vivaldi

(Italy, 1678–1741)

THE AUTUMN HUNT

Almost 300 years ago, in Italy, Antonio Vivaldi composed a collection of "sound-pictures" that magically brought seasonal sights and sounds to the ear. Naming his music *The Four Seasons*, he used violins to imitate bird calls for "Spring," swarms of wasps for "Summer," and icy winds for "Winter." In our piece, he delights us with trotting horses and hunters' horns for "The Autumn Hunt."

Light and lively